Define and Execute

Destiny S. Harris

...

. . .

Copyright

Copyright © 2024 Destiny S. Harris.

All rights reserved. No part of this publication may be reproduced without prior written permission from the author, except in the case of quotations.

Book design by Destiny S. Harris.

First printing edition 2024.

www.destinyh.com

. . .

. . .

A Gift For You

Thank you for taking the time to read this book. As a token of my appreciation, here is a gift to you.

I give away free books daily. Here's how to get your free books today:

Step 1: Visit

amazon.com/author/destinyharris

Step 2: Filter books by "Price: Low to High"

Step 3: Download available free eBooks

. . .

. . .

Table of Contents

. . .

. . .

Quick Bit

Thank you for taking the time to read this book.

My hope is that you leave at least 1% better than before you read this book and walk away with at least one takeaway.

I'd like to graciously ask that you help me by leaving a <u>review</u> of this book; your feedback helps me write better books and helps others get a glimpse of the book.

With Kindness,
Destiny

. . .

. . .

Write It Down

The first step with any goal is to write that shit down.

A goal not written down cannot manifest. An unwritten goal is simply a dream.

You are 70% more likely to reach a goal if you write it down.

If you place the goal somewhere visible that you see often, you increase the likelihood of accomplishing the goal even more.

What are your goals in every area of life? Write them all down.

Exercise: Write down your goals in every area.

. . .

. . .

Think Bigger

Before we go to the following steps, review the goals you've written down.

Now think about if there were no limits to your goals how might your current goals expand?

Exercise: Re-write your goals based on a higher level of thinking.

. . .

...

Think Even Bigger

Let's take it **ONE MORE STEP FURTHER.**

I want you to ask yourself if you are limiting yourself in any way. Are there fears and doubts preventing you from thinking bigger and stretching yourself?

Our most significant limitations are frequently self-imposed.

Don't limit yourself.

Reach for the stars and know they are just the starting point (if you believe it to be true).

Exercise: Re-write your goals and stretch yourself. Your goals should make you feel uneasy.

. . .

. . .

Get Specific

If you want a new job, what does this new job look and feel like? How is the culture? What is the pay? What is your relationship like with your boss and colleagues? How much flexibility and autonomy do you have in your day-to-day? What do you feel like after work each day? Do you dread going to work? Do you even go into a physical office? Get **extra** specific.

Exercise: Ensure your goals are extremely specific.

. . .

. . .

Define The Steps

What will it take for you to reach your goals?

Define the steps clearly. Write down every little, medium, and big detailed action that will go into the process, so you know precisely how to execute to make the goal a reality.

Exercise: Write down the detailed steps for your goals.

. . .

. . .

Set A Timeline

When do you desire to accomplish your goals? What is the ideal timeline? How long do you believe it will take to accomplish your goals?

Exercise: Set a timeline for each of your goals. You can even go as far as setting the actual clock time.

Example: By the 4 of January 2XXX @ 11:59 pm, I will have achieved the goal of (X).

. . .

...

Determine What You'll Sacrifice

Goals don't get accomplished by themselves, and you'll frequently have to give up something in return.

Where there is a reward, there must be sacrifice.

What are you willing to give up to achieve your goals? How early are you willing to wake up? What activities are you willing to cease engaging in? Where are you currently investing time and energy on less productive or unrelated goal tasks?

Everyone has plenty of time. Use it wisely to accomplish your goals.

Exercise: Write down everything you will sacrifice to achieve your goals.

. . .

. . .

Start

The only way to make progress on your goals is to start. If you never start, you will stay at the starting line.

Are you ready?

Exercise: Get started.

. . .

. . .

Don't Stop

Once you get started, it's easy to stop.

But you must avoid quitting on yourself, your dreams, and your goals.

Quitters don't win.

The consistent, persistent, resilient, and determined always arrive at the finish line.

It's painful to keep going, but the reward is sweeter. Much of the pain we avoid is the pain we need to reach heightened levels of being and success.

Exercise: Once you get started, don't stop.

. . .

. . .

Keep The End In Mind

What is your end goal? What do you desire to accomplish at the end of your life? Where do you see yourself in the long run? What is your ultimate purpose, vision, and plan for your life?

Keep all of these answers at the forefront of your mind.

Exercise: Review your goals daily, and always think about the end goal.

. . .

. . .

Thank You For Reading

Thank you for reading this book.

Stay loved, blessed, lucky, favored, aware, joyous, enlightened, and committed to bettering yourself.

. . .

. . .

The End.

. . .

. . .

About Destiny S. Harris

Destiny S. Harris' goal is to positively inspire, cultivate, elevate, and educate the minds of individuals across the globe through her writing.

Creating (whether books, courses, articles, poetry, or music) has always been Destiny's thing, not to mention health & fitness and all things entrepreneurial.

Destiny published her first book, "Beauty Secrets for Girls," at age 11 and her second book, "Don't Wait Until It's Too Late," at age 12.

Destiny obtained three degrees in Psychology, Political Science, & Women's Studies. She also started her own music teaching business at the age of 14, which she led for over ten years. In addition, she has been teaching academic, career, and personal development topics to thousands of students and readers since 2004.

Outside of writing, Destiny loves and enjoys many activities: reading, weightlifting, walking, biking, traveling, football (and sports in general), dogs, animals, food, classic movies, quality and new experiences, mountain and ocean views, sleeping, plants, and nature.

Check out her work, leave a review, share your thoughts with your friends and family, and participate in a movement: **Serving others through self-education (books).**

Complete the Steps To Get Free eBooks:

Step 1: Go to

amazon.com/author/destinyharris

Step 2: Filter books by "Price: Low to High"

Step 3: Download available free books

. . .

. . .

Connect W/ Destiny S. Harris

Please reach out and stay in touch. Start a conversation today @ destinyh.com

. . .

...

Free Gifts!

Access courses & free eBooks at the link below:

destinyh.com

Please Leave A Review

If this book impacts you in some way, please let me know by dropping a review on it.

I write better books with **your** input.

. . .

Tell Me What You Want

I've written many books, but if you don't see what you're looking for or need, get in touch with me via my website, articles, comments, or reviews, and let me know what you're looking for so I can create it for you. I'm here to serve.

Destiny

. . .

. . .